An Insightful Journal for the Spiritual Journey

1010

TRANSFORMATION

©2020 by Roni Hopkins
All rights reserved.
ISBN: 978-1-7349035-3-9

JOURNALS OF REALIZATION

"The only truth one could ever die for is the truth they themselves have become"

Roni Hopkins is the creator of *Journals of Realization,* which are a collection of unique journals that specialize in spirituality and consciousness. She has traveled the world, connecting with all walks of life and lives her purpose dedicated to assisting others on their journey. The creation of these journals reflect those experiences and bring a level of universal insight to ones own spiritual path. Journals of Realization encourages you to discover and express your truth, wisdom and ever evolving awareness throughout the pages and beyond them through our virtual discussions.

Every path reveals its truth within you.

www.RoniHopkins.com

PREFACE

When you suddenly find yourself on this Journey that is unknown, where you become unrecognizable to yourself and All seems too unreal to be true.

Where it shifts the way you relate to people, situations, outcomes and circumstances. You realize nothing was ever what it seemed to be and nothing will ever be the same.

And it is All Transformed right before your eyes

Spiritual Transformation is not a simple change in behavior, thought or action. It is a complete metamorphous of your entire existence. It creates a new way for you to approach, understand and live life on every level.

The Spirit, being the guiding force for all aspects of your life and the mind operating only secondary in nature. This process is different for everyone but one aspect is common amongst all, the entire system from once we use to operate becomes obsolete for something new to evolve.

This is the alchemy of the Spirit.

And the Spirit does this effortlessly when it is required for us to do so.

The spiritual journey is a complex one. It unveils and opens you to so much and leaves you realizing the truth of anything is subject to change. This change is the mechanism that everything is constantly woven into.

From time, to thought, to ideas, to growth, to all that adds to life in this physical world and the infinite universes

It all changes and transforms, taking on new embodiments, directions and placements in existence.

We are part of this universal flow and when we begin to see ourselves within this force as a natural creation from it, we have the ability to operate limitless within the limitations of time.

This is your Spiritual Journey

From Pen to Paper

Your Thoughts

Your Experiences

Your Realizations

"The unknown paths of the spirit can lead you through lifetimes in a single life"

The abundance of life the spirit holds is an unpredictable force that leads you through more life than you could imagine.

Experiencing Life beyond the layers

Writing the moments of your life with the vibrancy of a child's imagination and with every Yes, you are opening yourself to see just how immeasurable ALL of this existence really is.

The unknown is something you no longer fear, something you no longer lose control over but you embrace with acceptance and anticipation of all that the spirit can lead you through.

10 10

10 10

"The mind is to be free in thoughts and not controlled by them."

The process of spiritual transformation shifts the mind from its control of defining our reality. The mind, without spiritual awareness, is the platform from which every aspect of our human nature is perceived.

From our identity, ideas, beliefs, emotions, memories, perceptions and limitations

The mind is at the core of all of them.

The spirit oversees the mind and allows us to be free from our limitations of it. The mind begins to accept and operate from a position of conceptualizing from our spirit and allowing our thoughts to simply be of observance and not the only reality we once perceived from.

10 10

> "*Change comes to evolve each one of us in its own perfect timing.*"

Change is not a power that is to be imposed on others. Outside of your own realizations, it becomes an attempt to control someone else's existence, solely based on your perceptions of reality.

Each one of us holds our reality within the framework that life has presented it to us. The uniqueness is our own individual relationship to discover, experience, become and grow with all of life as it evolves us through this journey.

Life always presents us with new beginnings and in those beginnings each of us, in our time, will find our way through.

Your life is the only responsibility for you to do so.

Listen

Sometimes you can hear what can never be heard
And often times it is the heart

Shouting
Whispering
Panting

"Trust" it says

Purpose set with desires
To fulfill only what it was created to beat for

It is difficult to believe in something you have never heard
And it is misgiving to desire what you have never felt

But the heart knows
And you cannot deny it

Like love that is relentless to release
Speaking in between the here and now
The peace and the stillness

Of all that ever was
And all that everything is
The heart remains true to its calling

Silence the wondering mind
Displace fear where it no longer belongs

Hear between the beats
That moment, the second before it rushes to the next

You will hear it loud and clear
The heart setting you Free

10 10

"Spiritual Transformation is not something you choose or decide. It is completely outside of the realm of the mind."

Many have tried to induce such a transformation of life that goes beyond the control of what any of us could render.
The results are the purest of all treasures of life discovered.

What you begin to realize and possess is an invaluable existence that you quickly see as something that you could not have created within the scope of your abilities.

The existence of everything far exceeds our minds understanding to comprehend it and our spiritual journey sends us soaring into the realms beyond it.

It is the life that we all breathe for
The love that we seek forever in
The joy that remains in heartache
The peace in the eye of a storm

And once we find ourselves on this path, we can never go back.

10 10

10 10

"Who am I? Creates an answer that can never be."

The identity you perceive is an identity that is created from a world that requires everything to be defined as something.

Who you are at your core cannot be defined only experienced in this physical life. You are a constant being of eternity.

That identity is one that is consistently changing itself, allowing time to reveal all that you are, all that it is and all that it can create itself to be through you.

The Spirit recognizes itself in everything.

10 10

10 10

> "*Everything happens at the perfect time and Nothing can happen outside of it.*"

It is an influence that plays behind the scenes of life. It cannot be rushed forward or slowed down. If you ever find yourself trying to control it, you will find yourself being controlled by it.

And learning the patience of perfection

What is presented before you is all that you can live. Focus on living the most you possibly can with the present state given.

And know that everything is happening at the right time and exactly when you are supposed to be living it.

"The spirit flows from an eternal state of abundance which allows us to be in a constant state of fulfillment."

One cannot experience a fulfilled life if one does not recognize all of life itself, *is* fulfilled. Every part of life is created from this perfected point of creation. Your life's fulfillment comes through acceptance and without holding any expectations on how life does this for you.

The spirit exists from a state of wholeness, there is no lack in the true values of life. Even in scarcity, do we find the myriad of oneness flowing. When we begin to accept life beyond our limitations of it, we are free to experience all of life fulfilling itself through every moment of our lives.

It insures that no matter where you are in life, you are connected to the abundance source of which everything is created from and your life will comprise of all that it will ever need to fulfill it.

10 10

10 10

10 10

Undone

Tears fell and even though you have been here time and time again, each time was a reminder of why you should let go

Feel every struggle, feel every second of life pulling you, let the tiredness spread and consume your strongest parts

You are not okay and for once you can be okay with that

You believed you had arrived, believed you were on a path set in stone but you too faced a road block

One that required a detour into the unknown

Security holds no comfort to a weary soul and you suppose when all of this passes you will be better than you are now

As happiness only showed through your smile and deep down you knew there had to be more

For the life that you lived is fading in the background. A remembrance of all that once was, to be forgotten

Today of all days, the last piece that was holding you together finally came undone

Though dreams hold our faith in the stars and our hope in its imagination

Today, reality stood in front of you, reflected your identity and demanded for you to change

10 10

"Push beyond the boundaries of your previous state of being. Who you truly are is setting you free."

The most powerful aspect of spiritual transformation is that it sets your eternal, absolute existence free.

Anything that holds as a restriction to this freedom, your spirit rids all your existence from. It can be a daunting process that leaves you caught in-between a space of who you were and who you are to be.

As we are unaware of much of what is being transformed, only experiencing the process of it. Over time, more will be revealed and more will continuously be aligned.

10 10

10 10

"The mind is no longer the teacher but a student to what is Eternal."

The spiritual journey displaces the mind into unknown territory. It leaves the mind adapting to a new way to exist within your existence.

The mind does not know how to exist outside of what it knows.

The spirit is ever creating from the unknown, as this is the point that holds no boundaries to its freedom.

It takes time for the mind to adjust to this new way of existing, to learn from what it does not control and from a realm that is unfamiliar to its reality.

10 10

10 10

10 10

10 10

" The world suddenly becomes a destination where we are simply visiting to experience."

Everything is created to experience and explore the fullness of your life. Rather it is joy, despair, pain, happiness or sorrow. The world is a place for us to experience the nature of being human.

Nothing happens to you in the concept of life being set against you in any way

It all happens through you, as you, for you.

Every ending, we must find ourselves letting go and embracing the beginning with open arms. As this life is not a forever one but one that we all come and leave with our soul's journey lived.

10 10

10 10

10 10

10 10